THIS BOOK
IS PRESENTED
TO

_____

FROM

_____

MESSAGE

_____
_____
_____
_____
_____
_____

Handel

My Journey to a Better Life

Handel Dockery

authorHOUSE®

AuthorHouse™
1663 Liberty Drive
Bloomington, IN 47403
www.authorhouse.com
Phone: 1 (800) 839-8640

Published by AuthorHouse 04/06/2016

ISBN: 978-1-5246-0241-3 (sc)
ISBN: 978-1-5246-0240-6 (e)

Print information available on the last page.

Any people depicted in stock imagery provided by Thinkstock are models, and such images are being used for illustrative purposes only. Certain stock imagery © Thinkstock.

This book is printed on acid-free paper.

**Dedicated to my mother:
Mrs. Sarah Dockery**

PROLOGUE

EVERYONE HAS A STORY TO TELL. CERTAINLY, MANY who have left their places of birth in search of a seemingly better life in a foreign country have compelling stories to tell. Before I left my home country, I felt trapped. There were very few opportunities. As a young man, I was very naïve, albeit full of aspirations and dreams.

I longed to travel to America. I didn't understand why the warmth of sunshine, the beauty of foaming waves on sandy beaches, and the grace of swaying palm trees in my country seemed to instill joy, relaxation and calmness in foreign visitors.

Contrarily, I took those tropical features for granted because I felt restless, and longed to venture into a world of the unknown. Somehow, from far away on a small island, foreign lands seemed much more appealing to the spirit of youth.

Every young person I knew then, wanted to travel to America. From a distance, it was the land of endless opportunities - a place where dreams came true.

Leaving a broken home behind had set the stage for a brand new start. I had no idea that it was an adventure that would take me to places far beyond my wildest dreams, and nightmares. Being a frustrated teenager, foreign lands seemed the most viable option to escape the traps of poverty.

None of the adults who returned to the island on vacation spoke about the challenges that they experienced abroad. They all sported happy faces. They were well dressed, in fancy, expensive-looking clothing, and possessed lots of beautiful things.

It seemed that money wasn't a problem for those who were once poor (before they had left the island). The photographs they showed, and stories they told, though sometimes embellished, portrayed the picture of a better life abroad.

Many people returned just briefly, to visit family, or to attend an event. Whether the event was a happy one, like a wedding or a sad one, like a funeral, it didn't matter. Those who came from foreign lands looked more refined, and contented with the foreign way of life. They could hardly wait to return. I wanted that life too!

No one chose to tell about hardships, lest their tales of reality were shunned. Perhaps, no one on the island would believe them, because America was deemed the land where dreams came true. Back then, I couldn't imagine that life abroad would be worse than my experience of rural life on a small island. I was anxious to leave by any legal means necessary.

Although unsure of what readiness to leave felt like, I knew intuitively, that it was time for me to risk change. Like many other young men, I was willing to take a chance. I was convinced that luck of the draw could vary based on opportunities, and hard work. At least that was what I chose to believe then.

My Journey to a Better Life is the true story about my life as a young man who left his home in 1968, and headed to work on the sugarcane plantations in Belle Glade, Florida, U.S.A. I started on that journey to fulfill the dreams of a brand new life that would compensate for hardships of childhood.

Leaving that beautiful tropical island behind also meant seizing an opportunity to emerge from ashes like the phoenix, and fly away to find a new way of life. That new life was many miles away, in the foreign land of the rich and famous - America.

IN HINDSIGHT, THE YEAR 1968 WAS A TUMULTUOUS year for Americans, especially for people of African ancestry. It was the year that Dr. Martin Luther King Junior, leader of the Civil Rights Movement, was assassinated. African-Americans were asserting their civil and human rights for justice and equality.

Ironically, in the seventeenth and eighteenth centuries, Africans were seized against their wills from their homes, and shipped to America to work as slaves on plantations; there I was, in the twentieth century, voluntarily headed for America, to work on the sugarcane plantations.

That new journey led to a lot more than I could ever imagine or bargain for. It was the toughest test of my humanity and spirituality! Running from Jamaica was my plan, with big hopes of finding prosperity in America. My journey took me from dreams on a small, warm Caribbean island, to huge sugarcane plantations in America, to a cold reality in Canada.

My life went through many bizarre twists and turns, as I kept running. Working on the sugarcane plantations proved more challenging than I anticipated. Being thrown into circumstances where my survival hung by a thin thread, I threw caution to the wind. My life spiraled; I went in and out of jail, and was tossed in a world where I was often forced to make desperate choices. Some of those choices were unspeakable until now. Nonetheless, I kept on running!

This is the story of my coming of age without the guidance of a father, while escaping physical punishment from my mother. I battled a sometimes vicious world where all that glittered was not silver or gold, and maturing entailed huge risks, strong faith, and high stakes.

Through it all, I ran, I prayed, I cried, and sometimes, I laughed. On this journey to a better life, I felt despair, envisioned hope, and learned survival. Yet, my regrets are few. ***HANDEL - My Journey to a Better Life*** is *my* story.

PART ONE

CHAPTER ONE

IT WAS APRIL, 1973. DRESSED IMPECCABLY, WITH MY green tailored suit, shirt, tie, black leather shoes, and colourful knitted Tam (a hat that was made popular by the Rastafarians) and matching stick, I boarded a bus in the small town of Poughkeepsie, New York. As we approached the border in Buffalo at around 9 p.m., I retrieved my documents in preparation for entrance into Ontario, Canada.

For weeks, I had prepared for this trip. I had thoroughly memorized all the information that I thought would be requested, which was typical when entering a foreign country. I assumed that the Canadian immigration process would be pretty straightforward as when I had arrived in America in 1968; no passport was required for me to travel then.

After I had passed the selection process, in my country, I was given a farmer's ID card. If my recollection serves well, that card had an ID number, my name, and my country of origin - Jamaica. I had traveled to Belle Glade, West Palm Beach, Florida, America with many other men. We were hired to work on the sugarcane plantations, as part of the foreign farmers program.

In the summer of 1968, shortly after my arrival in Florida, I realized that cutting sugarcane was much more difficult than I had anticipated. Desperate to leave Jamaica, I had lied about my work experience. During the interview which was part of the selection process, I told the interviewer that I knew how to cut sugarcanes. After all, I was familiar with using a machete, and thought that the job would be easy.

However, my boss on the plantation soon realized that I was unable to keep up with the required pace of cutting the sugarcanes, unlike most of the other young men who finished their tasks in record time. Although I was not successful at cutting sugarcanes, I had accomplished my dream of being in America. I thought it was the only way of escaping poverty.

I had dodged attempts to send me back to my native island of Jamaica, and had continued to find ways to survive. I kept running from situations in order to escape death and lurking incarceration.

NOW, I WAS ABOUT TO EMBARK ON A BRAND NEW journey in pursuit of a chance to live in Canada. I had rehearsed that my reason for traveling to Canada was to attend the funeral of a relative. As proof, I had purchased a funeral wreath, and a new black, tailored suit, which I had carried in a suit bag. The journey was uneventful, and the hours seemed like days.

As the bus stopped at the Canadian border I tried my best to relax, but my breathing was not normal. The bus driver announced that all passengers should have their travel documents handy. There was silence, except for shuffling sounds as everyone retrieved their documents and waited. A white, uniformed immigration officer boarded the bus. The Canadian immigration officer asked that all passengers show their travel documents.

Slowly, he walked through the aisle and checked by glancing at the passports and Identification cards that were displayed by each passenger. I sat close to the back nervously awaiting my turn.

Then, I showed the immigration officer my ID. Upon examination of my travel document, he asked me to accompany him to the immigration office. Of all the passengers on that full capacity Greyhound bus, the officer had picked me! I was uncertain as to why I was the sore thumb.

Without comment or question, I followed the officer's command. All eyes were focused on me. I would be the reason for everyone's delay. My heart thumped loudly. The flow of adrenaline made me feel warm, despite the cold air, and the snow-covered ground. I tried to keep a straight posture.

It was unclear what triggered the officer's decision to flag me, of all the passengers on the bus. Was it the ID card, my skin colour, my multi-coloured hat and matching stick, or my attire? I was wearing a light coat, which was more suitable for spring.

When I left Poughkeepsie, it was an ordinary day in spring with clear, blue skies; I had no idea that winter still lingered in Canada. As I stepped off the bus, and looked down at the snow-covered ground, my thoughts were filled with a prayer.

Slowly, I mustered up the confidence to face my fate, with strong faith. I believed that I had the answers to whatever questions the immigration officer might pose. I had rehearsed all the possible questions and answers throughout the ten hour journey. Now, all I had to do was answer promptly with no jitters, and a straight face. Nervously, I anticipated pulling it off without a glitch.

Successful entry into Canada would provide the perfect escape from my troubles, and the opportunity for a new life. I was determined not to return to my shattered dreams in America where life had given me one nightmare after another.

As we entered the office, I stared blankly around the big room. It is difficult to recall all the details of that room now. However, while in the room, I noticed that the immigration officer who had boarded the bus was showing my ID to another immigration officer, and they seemed to be consulting with each other. I could not hear their conversation. Then, the other officer approached me. A glass panel separated us.

That officer looked at the ID card. He then proceeded to question me about: my reason for visiting Canada, my intended length of stay, and a list of the items that I was carrying on the trip. I answered smoothly that I was attending my father's funeral; I would be staying with relatives in Sudbury, Ontario, and I would be returning to America on the day after the funeral. I had one thousand US dollars cash in my wallet.

I felt certain that all my answers would meet the satisfaction of the officer's inquiry. As he paused to scrutinize the travel document again, I felt a surge of nervousness swelling inside me. It was difficult to remain quiet.

I blurted, "I am an American! Why are you asking me so many questions?" Calmly, the officer enquired if I had any additional ID. I retrieved a birth certificate and pushed it in the space underneath the glass panel. The birth certificate matched the name on the ID card. He scrutinized it, and then left to consult with another immigration officer.

Meanwhile, I waited with nerves that seemed to be getting the better of me. My body was perspiring profusely and my eyes wandered involuntarily around the room. Then I started to tremble, while in my mind, I prayed my favourite Bible verse: "The Lord is my Sheppard, I shall not want…" (Psalm 23 KJV).

CHAPTER TWO

As a child, my mother, a deeply religious, God-fearing woman had taught me to pray. Our family attended Evangelical church every Sunday. Service was very animated. It was the best day of the week, because it was the only day that I was allowed to dress up, and wear shoes.

On all the other days I had to walk bare-footed, whether I was attending school, or doing chores that included: fetching water from the pond, a mile away; gathering fire wood for cooking; feeding the chickens; tying out the goats; milking the cows; washing dishes; cooking, and taking out the garbage.

Life in the District of Haddo, in the Parish of Westmoreland, on the island of Jamaica, had become so frustrating and burdensome that just past my thirteenth birthday, I ran away. I had not planned to leave home but on that fateful day, my mother's physical punishment had pushed me over the edge.

That day, in her absence, I had prepared supper. I asked one of my younger siblings to wash the dishes and she refused. So I served her food in an unwashed plate. She cried, and refused to eat.

When my mother returned home, she was furious! She had accused me of acting as a grown up. That evening she had administered another beating, and challenged me to leave.

While administering lashes with a leather belt, she gave commands. Of course, then, I didn't understand it might have been her way of expressing frustration and disappointment. It had nothing to do with me, personally. Overtime her physical punishment became overbearing.

That day, in her Jamaican patois tongue, she scolded:

"You ah turn man 'pon me? If you t'ink you a man, den get out! Get you own place!"

Her husband (my father) had already abandoned our home, and lived in another parish with his next wife and family. I could recall that my father had visited us only once; I was a small child. My mother, who adhered to not 'sparing the rod, and spoiling the child,' was a very strict disciplinarian! I had grown tired of her punishment.

The next morning, about 4 a.m., while my mother and siblings were still asleep, I quickly packed my few belongings in a small grip (suitcase), and left home. I boarded a bus, and headed for the city of Montego Bay; it is the capital of the neighboring parish of St James.

Although Montego Bay was only a few miles away, the journey seemed very long that morning. The bus made several stops to pick up passengers who were on their way to work, or to sell fruits and vegetables at the market.

Living on my own, and seeking employment to survive had meant, hard work, and little pay. I had to mature quickly because choices were limited, and many of the grownups that I had encountered were abusive and deceitful.

I believed with all my heart that God kept his promises. Also, I was seriously bent on keeping the promise I'd made, just before the judge had granted me bail from jail in America. While in jail, I had made a pact with God. If He allowed me to get out of jail, I would be a changed man. I had promised God that I would serve him fervently; if I broke my promise, God's punishment would be to take my life.

As I stood waiting for the decision of the immigration authorities, I renewed that promise if God would help me to enter Canada. My situation had appeared grim because the immigration officer seemed to have sensed something was amiss. Maybe, he was trying to figure out whether my ID card and birth certificate were authentic documents. There was nothing I could think about that would warrant a denial of my entry to Canada. I had answered all the questions correctly.

After scrutinizing my travel documents, the immigration officer made another request. I had no way of anticipating that one; it was like what is called a 'bouncer' in the game of cricket. That was when the bowler did a tactical throw of the ball that often bounced off the pitch, and was aimed at hitting the batsman, or outing him. A bouncer was a very difficult ball to hit.

That situation, though tough, was no game, but it was a hard hit. Under nail-biting pressure, I stood impatiently looking at the immigration officer.   He seemed a bit hesitant. I sweated as I waited for him. Then he asked me to give him a sample of my signature. He put a piece of paper under the glass panel. I glanced at the paper.

Of all the information I'd memorized, and all the possible scenarios that I'd played out in my mind, I did not expect that request. It was a bouncer indeed; I was shocked.

"Officer, did you say my signature?"

"Yes sir."

I asked the immigration officer to repeat his request; I couldn't believe my ears! I had no idea what the signature on the document looked like. Although I had looked at the ID card several times, there was no way that I had the ability to do an accurate replica of the signature.

My guts churned, threatening to dispel its contents. My mouth produced a sour taste as the officer handed me a pen. My hand was visibly nervous. I had no recollection of what the signature on the travel document looked like, and from my nervous reaction, it was difficult to write even *my* signature.

The immigration officer stared at my tense face, and then at my trembling hand as I held the pen. He seemed confident that he had discovered an imposter. It would mean that he was competent in carrying out his duties for the Canadian authorities.

I had no idea if I would be able to replicate the signature on the ID card. As I placed the tip of the pen on the paper, beads of perspiration formed on my forehead. It seemed impossible to make a duplicate of something that I had no conscious memory of. With patience, the immigration officer stood there awaiting my response.

My hand was shaking from nervousness and fear. If only that officer had known my story, and had understood that I was drowning in desperation, maybe he would have found it in his heart to grant me entrance to a new life in Canada.

I couldn't force myself to tell him the truth, because I had known that the repercussions could be ruinous. As I was about to write the signature, it occurred to me that my fate was literally in *my* hands! As I held the pen that fateful day, at the Canadian border, my whole life seemed to flash before me.

CHAPTER THREE

I'D HAD A CHALLENGING LIFE. SINCE I WAS A SMALL child about four years old, my father had abandoned our family. I didn't even have a photo of him. Of course, back then cameras were a luxury that only the wealthy could afford.

I would always remember the last time that my father had visited; I was about six years old. That evening, our neighbour Solomon had come to our home with the news. My mum (whom everyone in our neighbourhood called 'Miss Neita'), was preparing dinner. He told her that Mr. Dockery was down the road, and wanted help to carry up some things.

My older siblings went to help that man; I didn't know who he was. He brought some food items: yams, dasheen, eddoes, etc.

When he arrived at our home, he looked at me and asked: "What's your name?"

I replied, "Handel, Sir."

Then he looked at my baby brother and remarked, "Then you must be 'Pee.'"

My father was a stranger. Nonetheless, I was excited because, on that day, he gave me a special gift: a chicken. Oh, I was so happy! It was the very first time that someone had given me something to call my own.

The evening passed and it was bedtime. While I was in bed that night I overheard my father and mother arguing in the room a partition away. It was years later that I understood the meaning of that tumult. The following morning I left for school. All day I thought about my chicken; she was going to lay eggs and have lots of chicks.

When I returned home from school, I could not find the chicken, and my father was gone. At first I had thought that somehow the string which was used to secure the chicken's leg to a tree got loose, and it ran away. I searched the yard and called out: "Che! Che! Che!" (That was how we called chickens).

When my mother came home from work I told her that my chicken was missing. My mother left to enquire about my chicken. She returned with the bad news. My father had taken back the chicken, and sold it. He'd taken back my gift! I couldn't describe the feeling that came over me as I cried. I felt upset and angry. As I grew older, the thought of what he'd done made me bitter.

Realizing that it was impossible to console me, my mother sought support from my Godmother. My Godmother was a very kind-hearted person. When she saw how sad I was about what my father had done, she gave me another chicken, and that replacement seemed to make things better.

It was the last time I had seen my father until many years later. His absence affected me, more than I could express in words. Over the years, the memory of my father faded. I had no other childhood recollection of him, not even a photograph. My first conscious recollection of his face was when I was thirty years old.

My mother had raised my siblings and me as a single parent. She was a very proud woman. Her motto was: "Don't beg, don't steal, and tell no one your struggles; deal with it."

In the district where I was raised, there was no other family with the last name Dockery. Even though we were poor, I was proud. My mother taught us self-respect. She was clear that we should always respect the family's name. Getting in trouble with the law was non-existent. However, as a boy, I got into day-to-day 'boys-will-be boys' mischief and harmless scuffles with my friends.

Sometimes my mother had a hard time providing food for her children, so we had no extra resources for celebrations or gifts. Birthdays were uneventful. There were no Christmas presents but the meal on Christmas day was a mouth-watering feast fit for royalty. I looked forward to it each year.

My mother had planted a garden that provided food to feed her children. She grew a variety of food: yams, sweet potatoes, bananas, eddoes, dasheen, and much more. She also reared chickens, goats, and cows that provided fresh milk. Sometimes she sold the animals in order to supplement her income.

Occasionally, she went to work on the neighbouring plantations. The small sums of money that she earned from seasonal work were barely enough to buy the basic necessities. However, for the most part, we were happy and healthy children. Except for the measles and the mumps, I had no major childhood illnesses.

Life was simple in our District. In our house, there were no electricity, indoor plumbing, or running water, but that was normal for most families in rural Jamaica back in those days. No one seemed to miss any of the modern amenities and electronic gadgets that are now commonplace, and which many take for granted nowadays. Communication from outside the District was mostly letters and in cases of emergency, telegrams.

One day, my mother received a telegram with news that her mother had died. It was sad to see my mother cry. She went away to attend the funeral. I had never known my grandmother, although I learned later that she resided many miles away in another District - Ashton. My mother had left her childhood District of Ashton when she got married to my father, and then moved to the District of Haddo where she raised her children.

In our home, we had no telephone or television. I would never forget the first time I viewed television; it was 1964. I was fifteen years old, and I was at a friend's house in Montego Bay. That event was well publicized. I was in the company of a large group.

It was the first professional championship boxing match with Mohammed Ali (known then as Mr. Cassius Clay), when he defeated Mr. Sonny Liston who was the world's heavyweight champion prior. Mr. Liston had failed to respond to the bell at the seventh round. Clay won the fight; it was a technical knockout!

IN HADDO, THE BACKYARDS AND STREETS WERE OUR playgrounds. I enjoyed playing a variety of games such as hide-and-seek, tag, marbles, and cricket. It was fun, and a great way to combat boredom and make the time fly. I also hunted birds with my friends; we used slingshots and stones. My catch of a variety of birds made tasty roasts which we enjoyed eating.

As a young man, I longed for a better life. On that day when I ran away from my home in the District of Haddo in Westmoreland, Jamaica, I had no idea what awaited me in the city of Montego Bay. I had no known relatives or friends there. As I boarded the bus, my energy was fueled by fear and anticipation.

CHAPTER FOUR

THE BUS RIDE SEEMED VERY LONG DUE TO THE constant stops as the driver picked up passengers along the way. Some of the passengers were regular workers, and others were farmers who sold fruits, vegetables, and ground provisions at the market.

When the bus arrived in Montego Bay, I alighted like everyone else. Immediately, I started walking around from door to door enquiring about work.

My first job offer was from the owner of a Cabinet shop. The boss, Mr. Mud, hired me on the spot. My job was to sweep the dust and woodchips from the floor. I had no lunch, or money to buy lunch that day.

While the other workers left for lunch I lingered in the store. Mr. Mud observed that I had nothing to eat or drink. He offered me lunch. I gladly accepted; I was hungry. He asked where I was from and during our conversation I spoke candidly about the life that I ran away from, miles away in the District of Haddo, Westmoreland.

Mr. Mud listened intently. When he realized that I was a stranger to Montego Bay, he asked if I had any place to sleep that night; I told him no. He invited me to his home. At the end of the day he took me to a restaurant, and bought food; we ate dinner together.

Over dinner, he offered to buy me a motorcycle so that I could travel back to my home if I desired. I was cautiously happy that my new boss would be so generous - I didn't even know how to ride a motorcycle.

After dinner, Mr. Mud suggested that I stay in his room. He didn't take me to a house; instead, he took me to a room in the motel where we had just finished having dinner. He explained that the motel was his temporary home, since he was from the Bahamas. The only furniture in the room was a chair, desk, and bed. I lay on the bed and he came into the bed beside me. I felt uncomfortable, to say the least.

He then moved closer, and started rubbing my leg; I was scared. I pushed his hand away. I knew what he was doing was wrong. He ignored me and proceeded to place his hand between my legs. I screamed at the top of my lungs!

I startled him. In an effort to silence me, he put his hand over my mouth. I pushed his hand away, and screamed louder. Fearing that my screams would alert others, he retreated and spent the rest of the night on the chair.

The next day, I informed Mr. Mud that I no longer wanted to work for him, and that I needed payment for the day I had worked. He told me that I had worked for only half day, and offered me compensation of three shillings. I turned down his offer and demanded payment of three pounds.

He was furious, and refused. I continued to demand three pounds and he refused again. I then threatened to tell the other workers what he had done in the motel room the night before.

Knowing that his behaviour was not acceptable, I knew he didn't want to risk tarnishing his reputation. If his conduct toward me was exposed to the public, the repercussions would be serious and could even result in his death. Back then, any man accused of homosexual behavior or, as in my case, attempted homosexual assault, would be treated as an outcast.

I knew that Mr. Mud wouldn't want to risk having his inappropriate behavior toward me known to his staff, or anyone in the community for that matter. Without further argument, he paid me three pounds. That was a lot of money! With three pounds, I rented a room, and bought food.

I searched for another job. A few days later, I was hired at a restaurant. My duties included cleaning the floors, and washing the pots, pans, and dishes. Then, one day, while I was in the kitchen I observed the Chef as he seasoned meat. I was appalled at the amount of seasoning he used! I commented that he was using too much spice.

The Chef was angry that I had criticized his culinary skills. He chased me out of the kitchen. Then he complained to Ted, the restaurant owner, and suggested that I should be fired for my insolence. Upon investigation, Ted learned what had happened and questioned my ability to cook. I told him that I knew how to cook.

He challenged me by asking that I prepare a steak for him that evening. He instructed the Chef not to assist me in any way. I prepared the steak and brought it to him. Ted was very impressed with my meal and asked where I'd learned to cook. I told him that I had attended classes at the prestigious Wiki Waki Club. I had only heard of that Club, where employees were taught to cook professionally, but I had never worked there. My intention, of course, was to make a great impression on my new Boss. I knew I succeeded because Ted then informed the Chef that I would be preparing meals for the restaurant the following day.

The Chef was so upset that he walked off the job and never returned. Immediately, I was promoted to the position as the new Chef. I remained in that job for about three years. It turned out to be my best paying job in Jamaica. That job provided a wealth of experience. Ted was very pleased.

During that time, I matured beyond my years. I mended the rift with my mother, and visited her when I had spare time. Although I never returned home to live, I gave her money whenever I could.

Overtime, word spread about my culinary skills and one day I heard about a position that was available in a new fancy restaurant on the other side of the city. I decided to pursue the vacancy since that was a much bigger restaurant and the wages would be better.

I felt confident that I would be hired. With the haste of youth, and the excitement of a new job that would provide me with a bigger income, I gave Ted notice of my resignation and moved on.

After my initial interview, I was hired. I then bragged to a friend about my new job in that fancy restaurant. I was offered the job, and I was scheduled to start working the following week.

However, my friend advised me to take extra measures to *keep* that new job. He suggested that I explore means to 'tie' myself in the job. I wasn't sure what he meant, but the thought of landing that job, and getting the guarantee to keep it was enticing.

On my friend's recommendation, I agreed to pay an inconspicuous visit to a man whom he introduced me to. This man, Mr. Finger, claimed that he had the power to place me permanently in the new job at the fancy restaurant.

My friend had exposed me to a new world of strange beliefs and rituals. I was skeptical, but curious especially as it promised to help me keep that new job, so I went along with his plan.

When we arrived at Mr. Finger's house, I noticed a Bible and a deck of cards on a table. Mr. Fingers explained that he would help me to keep the new job - there was no way I could be fired. It sounded too good to be true, but my friend had guaranteed that it would be worth a try.

Reluctantly I agreed, and paid the fees that Mr. Finger required for his services. I had heard of these types of people; some called them spiritualists, some call them seers. Mr. Finger gave me a small bottle of sweet-smelling, brown powder. He asked me to purchase a white handkerchief; it had to be brand new.

His instructions were as follows: on the first day, before I reported to work at the new job, I had to sprinkle some of the powder on the handkerchief, then put the handkerchief in my pocket, and walk backwards through the door from my house.

On my initial day of work at the new job, I had to meet with the manager of the new restaurant for a job orientation. As I entered his office, he greeted me. I did not respond to his greeting; instead I followed Mr. Finger's advice: I removed the white handkerchief from my pocket, and wiped my face. Without hesitation, the manager, as if familiar with that ritual, said, "So you are involved in those things too? Go home, I don't need you!"

There was no further conversation. I left. Needless to mention, I did not get that job. I was devastated! Again, I was unemployed. I went from door to door seeking a job. It took me a long time to find work, but eventually I was offered a job at a tailor's shop.

Briefly, I considered the idea of learning the skills of that trade. However, my job was to keep the floors clean and to run errands for the tailor. Business was slow, and my wages were not enough to pay all my bills.

I searched for a part-time job. I was hired to sell peanuts. It was hard work and the pay I received was based on my sales. The warm air from the cart made a whistling sound which alerted customers that packages of warm peanuts were on sale, as I pushed the cart around the city of Montego Bay.

Although the tailor didn't pay much money, he acknowledged that I was a diligent worker. One day, he asked if I was interested in traveling to America to work on the farms.

It seemed that, finally, God had answered my prayers. I expressed my interest with excitement. The tailor told me that he had a friend who was part of the recruiting process for men to work on the farms, in America, and he promised to help me. I had no idea how long that opportunity would take to manifest, but I was happy.

It became too difficult to live on the money that I received from the tailor shop and the sale of peanuts. I had to stay with a friend because I couldn't afford to pay rent. So after about a year, I resumed my search for more gainful employment. I got hired to load and unload a delivery truck. It was strenuous work but the wages were better.

Every morning of the week, the truck left Montego Bay, headed for Kingston, the capital city. There we loaded the truck with bags of dried goods such as flour, and rice, and sometimes animal feed. We then headed back to Montego Bay and delivered the goods to retail shops in and around the city.

For about two years we repeated that routine. I continued to pray for a lucky break. Later, to my delight, the tailor's friend contacted me about going to work in America. It was the light I awaited at the end of the tunnel.

CHAPTER FIVE

IN 1968, THE OPPORTUNITY TO TRAVEL TO AMERICA finally came. It was the answer to my prayers and the chance to get rich. I had thought that America was a country where the streets were paved with gold.

The tailor, my old Boss, had kept his promise to help me. His friend came to my house to deliver the great news. The gentleman gave me an invitation card to try out for the farm program. The card had my name and an address in Montego Bay where I had to take a test. As instructed, I went to that address to take a hand test. Back then, I had no idea that I would one day be traveling to Canada. My goal was to travel to America.

The hand test would determine whether my hands could withstand the physical challenges required for work on the sugarcane plantations in Florida. It meant that my hands had to be tough, evidenced by hardened, rough skin. I nervously allowed the examiner to touch the palm of my hands. Maybe the scratches and calluses inflicted by the loading and unloading of rough bags from my work on the truck had been a blessing in disguise; it paid off. I passed the hand test!

The interviewer then asked my age. Although the answer was straightforward, I lied. I told him that I was twenty-five years old.

He repeated the question: "How old are you?"

I told him that I was twenty-one years old. I was asked that questions three times before I gave him the correct answer. I was afraid that my age would disqualify me.

Somehow, the interviewer knew my age and, maybe, this was his way of testing my honesty. I finally gave him the correct answer after he said jokingly: "Boy, I can still see your mother's milk on your face."

Out of fear that I would be considered too young, to travel to America to work on the sugarcane plantations, I had tried to appear older. Actually, I was only nineteen years old.

I had reasoned that having lived on my own, and worked to support myself for almost six years, qualified me as a grown man. I had passed my mother's dare when she had challenged me to act as a man. Since I had run away from home at age thirteen years old, I had managed to provide food and shelter for myself.

Despite the lies about my age, the man had determined that my hands were tough enough for the plantation job. He saw my enthusiasm and decided to afford me the opportunity to fulfill my dreams of traveling to America.

However, he did not have the final say. I had to do another test. He gave me the okay for advancement to the second stage of the recruitment process. For that stage, I had to travel to the city of Kingston. There I underwent physical and medical testing. I passed again.

The final step was to receive my Identification card. In lieu of a passport, that special card was issued. My recollection of the information printed on that ID card was my name, a number, and a photo of my face. It was for use solely to travel to America to work on the sugarcane plantations with one employer for a specified period of time. It was not transferable or renewable.

On the day that I boarded the flight to America, I bid farewell to Jamaica and my miserable past. It seemed like an ordinary day with sunshine and blue skies as the plane ascended. I was excited! I was filled with anticipation of a new life. I had dreams of becoming rich, and having a much easier life.

I had very little idea what the foreign farm program was about. Essentially, I understood that it was an arrangement between the American and Jamaican labour authorities. I had figured that working on a sugarcane plantation in America couldn't be that difficult. I had reasoned that cutting sugarcanes was simply the means to an end. Entering America under any legal circumstances was a stepping stone to an opportunity for a new life.

There was no way that I would even entertain the idea of returning to a life that seemed empty. I had left nothing that I wanted to reclaim. Prior to leaving Jamaica, I had given away all of my possessions, except for the few items that I had packed to travel.

My friend back in Montego Bay was happy to receive a new brood of chickens, my bedroom set and a few other pieces of furniture, some pots and pans, and my coal pot. The coal pot was a devise made out of cast iron, and operated by charcoal (from burnt wood) and used for cooking.

The plane landed in West Palm Beach, Florida, and along with the other men I was transported to Belle Glade, Florida. My new home was a camp; it was special housing which the American company had prepared to house foreign workers who worked on the farm program.

The camp was a large two-storey building. The administration office was on the ground floor, and the dormitory was on the top floor. The dormitory was a big open room that housed many farm workers who slept on bunk beds; two men per bed. A separate building that housed the kitchen and dining room was in close proximity to the building that housed the dormitory.

Breakfast was served by the kitchen staff every morning. All the workers lined up to receive a meal. After breakfast, around 8 a.m., all the workers were transported from the camp to the sugarcane fields. Lunch was served on the sugarcane field; the daily menu was rice and pork.

Every worker was equipped with a machete to cut two rows of sugarcane, and shin guards for protection. We worked alongside each other. Once a worker finished cutting two rows, he was assigned additional rows at a different field.

Some of the other workers were experienced because they were returning, having worked on the sugarcane plantations previously. It was my first experience; I was a rookie. My performance lacked the necessary skills to cut sugarcanes quickly, so I was unable to complete my rows. Being alone in the field, I felt lonely. All the other workers completed their rows, and left me by myself.

We had weekends off, for relaxing and shopping. During my time off, I would hang out with my friend Tim, from Montego Bay. We'd met in Kingston and had traveled together to work on the sugarcane plantations in Belle Glade, Florida. Soon, he had devised a plan to run away from the camp.

Tim had two uncles in America; I'll call them Jeff and Shane. Jeff resided in Florida, and Shane resided in Connecticut. Jeff sold clothing to farm workers in the evenings; he traveled to various camps to sell and took Tim with him to help out.

Since Tim and I were friends, I tagged along with him and his uncle. Soon, Jeff and I became familiar with each other. Jeff and Shane had decided to smuggle Tim away from the farm. They came up with a plan, and needed help.

We were aware that it would be difficult, or near to impossible for Tim to escape the camp because the rules were very strict. In fact Joe, the camp's supervisor, conducted a head count every night at bedtime. He would check to ensure that every person was in bed.

Reluctantly, I had agreed to help with Tim's escape. On the night that we executed the plan I was nervous. Joe entered the room to make his rounds, and as usual, he checked all the beds. At first I laid in Tim's bed, pretending to be him. Right after the supervisor checked on me (thinking that I was Tim), I quickly got up from my friend's bed. As Joe walked through the dormitory, I hurried to my bed. Unknowingly, he checked me a second time.

Tim's escape-mission went well. He was quietly whisked away by his uncle Shane, without any commotion. Tim left for Connecticut with his uncle that night.

The next morning, after breakfast, when the camp authorities found out that my friend was missing, they mounted a search. Tim was nowhere to be found! I was questioned about his whereabouts. I was uncertain why they had chosen to target me because I had not discussed Tim's escape plan with anyone.

I guess because Tim and I were close friends, someone may have told Joe that I had known something. Tim never returned to the camp.

One day while I was working on the farm, I was feeling very depressed; it was a lonely feeling. Everyone had left me in the field. I realized that I couldn't do the job. It was lunchtime and the boss was coming with lunch.

As the truck approached, I sat down and pretended to be ill. I thought illness would be a way to escape the field. I complained to the supervisor that I had been experiencing severe back pains, and headaches. I was taken to the hospital, and there the doctor recommended that I rest for a week before returning to work.

While I was on sick leave, I stayed all day at the camp. After everyone had left for work, I went to a nearby Department store, and enquired about a job. The owner of the store hired me to paint the walls for 65 cents per hour.

Accepting that job was a crucial mistake because another farm worker saw me working, and reported me to the supervisor. Working outside the farm was considered a breach of contract; it was called "draw joint." This illegal action could result in deportation. Consequently, the supervisor notified me that I would be transferred from Belle Glade to work on another farm in Okeelanta.

Previously, I had overheard that workers from Okeelanta were being transferred to Belle Glade to work. Also, there was a rumour that there was insufficient work on the farms in Okeelanta. It didn't make sense that they would be transferring me from Belle Glade to Okeelanta at that time. I was very suspicious.

I asked Joe if he would pay my wages for the work that I had done before I was transferred to Okeelanta. He informed me that I would be paid on my return to Jamaica.

He said: "Return to Jamaica!"

It must have been a slip of Joe's tongue. He proved that my qualms were accurate. Inadvertently, my supervisor had confirmed that my suspicions were correct. The real plan was to deport me to Jamaica that morning, and not to transfer me to Okeelanta, Florida as he had previously indicated.

That day, when the 'transfer' to Okeelanta was scheduled to take place, I was summoned to the office via the intercom at the camp. I knew that they were planning to deport me to Jamaica, when I was instructed to return the shin guard and the machete, and to pack my trunk. Nonetheless, I proceeded upstairs to pack my belongings as instructed.

Without a plan, I was scared and nervous. I had to think quickly because I did not want to return to Jamaica. I was alone! Unlike Tim, I had no relatives in America to help me escape.

I ran upstairs to the dormitory and packed my trunk. However, I left it in the room, and told one of my co- workers that he could help himself to what was in the trunk after I left. I had also confided in him that I suspected that plans were underway to send me back to Jamaica. He expressed concern about my wellbeing. I had no place to stay, and I had only one dollar in my pocket.

Shortly afterward, I was called over the intercom, and instructed to report to the office immediately. As I looked downstairs I saw the bus. I knew that it was there to take me to the airport. So I went downstairs without my trunk. Joe asked me to return to the dormitory to retrieve my trunk, and return to his office.

CHAPTER SIX

IN MY GUT, I KNEW THAT RETURNING TO JAMAICA would never be a viable option for me. My dream of being in America was about to be shattered. I ran from a hard life in Jamaica! I had no idea that I would be running from America too, and not the slightest thought of escaping to Canada.

Joe waited in his office with the intention of deporting me to Jamaica. Without another word I turned around quickly, and left the office as if headed back upstairs to the dormitory.

However, instead of returning to the dormitory, to collect my trunk, I ran down the next set of stairs which led to the street. As soon as I got outside, I started to run, although I had no idea where I was headed. I kept on running!

Knowing that Joe would realize that I was missing, and call the authorities to find me, I had to get off the street. I had no escape plan! I ran through the first sugarcane field in sight.

Although I had no sense of direction as to where I was going, I just kept running through the green sugar cane fields. Green sugarcane fields were dangerous because they contained poisonous snakes, unlike burnt fields where fire was used to clear the snakes.

I was hot, exhausted and hungry, but I kept running. I was adamant that I would rather risk being bitten by poisonous snakes in the sugarcane field and even death, rather than return to Jamaica! I wanted to leave the past behind.

Back in Jamaica, I'd had two brushes with death. The first incident happened while I was in Montego Bay (just before I was hired to load the truck). I was staying with my friends because I couldn't afford to pay rent. One night, gangsters came and opened fire at my friend's house. They fired many shots through the windows and doors of the little wooden house. I thought I was going to die! We escaped through a window and ran down in the bushes to a nearby ravine. I was lucky to be alive!

The other incident occurred while I witnessed a dominoes game. One of my friends was gambling; he was winning. His opponent accused me of helping my friend with his game, but I was only watching them play. My friend's opponent lost the game and in anger, he stabbed me in my chest with a switchblade.

I was taken to the hospital with life-threatening wounds. However, no charges were laid, because the police were not informed. If I had chosen to report the incident, it would mean taking the dreaded risk of being a snitch. The penalty for snitching to police was a greater risk on my life.

In a frantic effort to escape deportation to Jamaica, I ran for several miles, and then I slowed down. I glanced at my wristwatch; it was midday. All around me was green sugarcanes that stretched in every direction. I decided then to follow a track out of the sugarcane field. To my surprise, I noticed a long lineup of men. I realized that it was another farmers' camp. So I went over and joined the line.

Recognizing that I was a stranger to their Camp, a few of the men enquired where I was from. I showed them my farm workers' ID card which indicated that I was from Belle Glade. I had no idea where I was until one of the men in the line asked: "What are you doing in South Bay?"

I replied sharply that I was in South Bay for shopping. I had lunch at the Camp and later I hung around the town to pass the time. I was a bit relieved, knowing that I had escaped Belle Glade. Later that evening at around 5 p.m., I returned to the South Bay Camp for dinner.

When some of the workers at the South Bay Camp enquired why I was still in town, I told them that I had missed the bus back to Belle Glade. After dinner I played a few games of Dominoes with a couple of the workers.

That night I had no place to sleep, and no money, except for that one U.S dollar. I also had no idea where I would sleep that night! Out of desperation, I had thought that maybe if I met a woman, she would take me home to sleep.

I started walking around the neighbourhood, searching for a place to spend the night. After a short while, I heard the sound of a machine; it was a lawnmower. Behind an enclosure, I saw a young woman mowing the lawn. I threw a small pebble to get her attention. When she turned around, I beckoned her to come near.

She approached me from behind the fence, and I introduced myself as Hartley Smith. She asked where I was from, and I told her that I was from Miami. She asked what I was doing in South Bay and I told her that I was on business for my job. She asked where I was staying and I told her that I was at the Holiday Inn. I wasn't aware that there was no Holiday Inn in that area.

She asked: "Which Holiday Inn? In Orlando?"

I replied: "Yes."

We kept talking, and she asked if I would like to meet her mum. She went into the house and returned with her mother. She introduced me to her mother. After a lengthy conversation, her mother asked her: "Do you want him to meet your dad?"

She replied, "Yes."

When he came out, to my astonishment, I recognized the man as Jeff. I could hardly believe my eyes when I realized that her husband was one of the uncles of my friend Tim, whom I had helped to escape from the Camp in Belle Glade.

Jeff and I stared at each other looking surprised, as his wife tried to introduce me as Hartley. He acknowledged me:

"This is Handel from Belle Glade; he is working on the farm."

Of course, I was embarrassed at the family knowing that I had lied about my name, and being from Miami. Jeff asked how I knew his address. I had no idea prior, that it was where he lived. One could say that it was a stroke of luck, divine guidance, or just coincidence I had stopped at that house.

Jeff invited me in, and I felt embarrassed about the lie I had told to his daughter and wife earlier that evening. I told Jeff about how I was questioned when his nephew escaped from the camp, and that I too was running away.

I explained that in desperation, I was trying to meet a young lady to take me in for the night. It was pure coincidence that I had ended up at his house. Jokingly, he told me that his daughter was a minor, only fifteen years old, and I should leave her alone. He invited me in his home. We chatted for a while.

Later he drove me to a rooming house in the South Bay area and paid for my room. He asked me to get ready the next day if I wanted to start work on a new farm. His job was to recruit workers for the vegetable farms – no ID was required.

The following morning, Jeff met me and took me to work on a new job site in the South Bay area. Alongside other workers, my job was to pick tomatoes, cucumbers, peppers, pickles, and onions. I also worked in the corn fields, plucking corn. I worked on various farms all summer.

The routine was that Jeff's bus would pick me up every morning and take me, and other workers (Americans), to the fields. He returned in the evening to take me back to the rooming house.

From time to time there were road blocks. The police and immigration authorities would pull over buses to do random searches. On those occasions everyone in the bus was asked to show proper ID. My only ID was the one that was issued from the Belle Glade Camp. It would not be considered valid by the authorities.

One morning on my way to work there was a road block. Jeff alerted me of the immigration. Just as he was slowing down, preparing to stop, I opened the door of the bus and began to run. The officers were in hot pursuit of me. They chased me, and I kept running. In my mind, I knew that in order to escape, I had to run to the sugarcane field. Once I entered the green sugarcane field they retreated.

However, I kept running through the green sugarcane field, without looking back.

CHAPTER SEVEN

IT WAS HOT, AND I FELT TIRED AND THIRSTY. THE energy from fear kept me going. Suddenly, the field ended with a narrow track. I followed the track which led me to the edge of a busy highway!

Cautiously, I crossed that highway which led to a parallel highway. Again I crossed over warily. Then, to my shock, I saw Jeff's bus. That was more than a stroke of good luck! Jeff recognized me; he seemed very surprised to see me.

I had no idea where I was. He stopped and asked what I was doing there. I explained that I ran, and had kept running through the green sugarcane fields in an effort to get away from the officers that were chasing me, earlier that day, but I had no idea where I was headed. He drove me back to work. I felt thankful to be rescued.

I continued to work on vegetable farms in Florida for the rest of that summer with no interruptions. I also worked on apple orchards in Orlando, Florida.

Later I worked on the Mule Train in the cornfields. The Mule Train was like a huge tractor with airplane-like wings that was used in the corn fields. After plucking ears of corn they were loaded into the Mule Train.

Then, at the beginning of autumn 1968, I got the opportunity to work on the apple farms. I left Florida with two of my American friends via the Greyhound bus, and headed to Salem, New Jersey.

Sharing a room with my two friends, I was housed in close proximity of the apple farm. We shared a kitchen and prepared our own meals. In addition to the job of picking apples, the farm also had work in the refinery indoors. There, the apples were put on conveyor belts and they were graded. I wanted to work in the refinery.

While my American roommate and I were standing in line to apply for employment at the refinery, I learned that a Social Security number was a requirement to be considered for the job. Jokingly, I snatched the document from my friend who was ahead of me in the line.

Taking a quick look at his document, I realized that the Social Security ID had nine numbers. I filled out my job application using a social security number that I composed with nine random numbers. By the time I got to the top of the line, and it was my turn to submit an application for a job in the refinery, I was asked for my Social Security ID and I told the recruiter that I had forgotten it at home. I was hired at the refinery.

Working at the refinery in New Jersey was great! Soon, I mastered the skills to work efficiently. Some of the workers were annoyed at my competence to say the least. Then one day, an argument with another worker resulted in a fist fight. As the fight escalated, I grew fearful that the police would be called. I ran away from the job and never returned.

In a hurry, I boarded the Greyhound bus to New Paltz, New York. There I worked on another apple farm. To my delight, that job had much better living arrangements. The company provided free accommodations with more privacy. I lived in a house with two other men. We shared kitchen and bathroom, but had individual bedrooms.

Life in New Paltz was much more relaxed. I made new friends, and went to parties. Sometimes we traveled to the neighbouring town of Poughkeepsie, about twelve miles away. One evening, at a party in Poughkeepsie, while at the bar, I met Pam, a woman who caught my attention. I introduced myself, and shortly afterward, we started going out together. That special lady lived with her mother and stepfather.

As our relationship grew, I moved in with Pam and her parents. When the apple-picking season was over, I went to work at a candy factory. Unfortunately, one day my hand was injured in the candy-making machine, and I was unable to continue working. I didn't return to work after my hand healed.

My next job was at a newspaper printing factory. I was the only person of colour at the company, and my role was to sweep the floors, and to bundle the newspapers for distribution. One day, while in the quality control room, I observed that a large quantity of newspapers was flawed. I brought it to the attention of the production manager.

Consequently, the manager offered me a job to work in the quality control room. The man who had held that job previously was assigned to my old job. As anticipated, he was unhappy with that switch, which resulted in his demotion.

We argued one day; he called me a "nigger"! I was furious. A fistfight ensued and in an effort to avoid defeat, I hit him with a wooden plank. When he fell to the floor, I panicked and ran away. I didn't return to my job at the newspaper.

In Poughkeepsie, I found work in construction as a general labourer with a building constructor. My job was to mix and pour concrete. It was hard work but my life improved and I earned decent wages.

One day, during one of my trips to New York City, a street vendor hustled me to purchase a diamond ring. We went back and forth as I negotiated a reasonable price. The street vendor's initial asking price of one thousand U.S. dollars shriveled to one hundred U.S. dollars. I thought it was a great bargain so I bought it, even though I had not planned to purchase jewelry on that trip. I bought the ring because it was a great deal. When I returned to Poughkeepsie, I gave it to Pam as a gift, without any ceremony, declaration or promises.

After receiving the gift, without my knowledge, Pam announced our 'engagement' to her family. Somehow, the significance of the diamond ring was misconstrued by my girlfriend. To my surprise, her relatives and friends threw an elaborate 'engagement' party.

I attended the party, not knowing that it was suppose to be a celebration of my engagement. During the party, Pam was asked about setting a date for the wedding. It was when I decided to disclose that it was a misunderstanding because I had not proposed marriage to her.

In hindsight, my remark was untactful; bad timing! Pam was embarrassed. As a result, we fought, and the relationship ended abruptly. Undoubtedly, I knew that at the age of twenty-one, I was not ready to get married, and settle down. I moved out and rented a room on my own.

My new room was on the first floor of a house. I had a separate kitchen, and I prepared my own meals. My landlady, Mrs. Clarke lived in the same house with her teenage daughter, Cherry. Cherry was a pretty fair-skinned girl, of medium height, with black hair. Shortly after I moved in, she demanded my attention. From all accounts, it became obvious to me that she was a promiscuous girl. I ignored both her blatant and subtle sexual advances. She did not handle my rejection well.

Mrs. Clarke had a friend who visited the house often. That friend, Mrs. Smith also had a sixteen-year-old daughter, Nikki, who was Cherry's friend. Sometimes Cherry had sleepovers at the house, and invited Nikki. I found Nikki intelligent, and a lot more 'normal' than her promiscuous friend. Often Nikki and I had lengthy, interesting conversations in my kitchen.

Upset about me consistently ignoring her daughter's advances, Mrs. Clarke decided that she would retaliate. Cherry hated being scorned, and she was jealous of her friend, whom I had chosen to converse with. Mrs. Clarke then told Mrs. Smith that I was locked in my room all day with her sixteen year old daughter, Nikki. I had no physical contact with that girl!

However, the lies that Nikki had been in my bedroom all day spread, and reached her father. Mr. Smith was enraged! He sent out a threat that he would kill me. Upon hearing about the threat from Nikki, I ran to a friend's house for rescue. I was scared for my life!

After serious consideration of the consequences of running away, I decided to return and confront the situation to prove my innocence. I thought that by leaving I would give the wrong impression, and some people, including Nikki's father, a gun owner, would believe the allegation.

Upon returning to house, I stood on the sidewalk and I observed Nikki coming down the stairs; I caught her attention. She asked:

"What are you doing here? My dad is upstairs with a forty-five (handgun)."

She asked me to leave because her dad was planning to kill me. I refused to leave. I then asked her to go upstairs and tell her mother to come down with her; I also instructed her not to tell her mother that I was there.

When Mrs. Smith came downstairs to meet me, I introduced myself. Then I told her that the allegations about me and Nikki were false because we were never in a closed room. I informed her that my mother had raised me to respect young women, and to keep my hands to myself. I also told her I had heard the rumour that her husband was planning to kill me.

Then, although I was scared I expressed my desire to speak with Mr. Smith. She listened. Mrs. Smith seemed very impressed with my honesty. I then asked her to bring her husband to meet with me. I also requested that she not let Mr. Smith know that I was waiting.

CHAPTER EIGHT

I INTRODUCED MYSELF TO MR. SMITH. HE WAS A short, dark-skinned African-American man. When he realized who I was, he pulled out a handgun from his pocket. I asked him to give me the opportunity to explain the truth before he used his weapon. I told him that I heard he had plans to shoot me because of the lies he was told regarding his daughter and me.

I was sweating profusely, but I felt proud that I was able to stand in my truth, regardless of the consequences. Running away would give the impression that I had done wrong, or had something to hide or be ashamed of.

Nervously, I explained to the girl's father, that I didn't have a personal relationship with his daughter. I told him that I liked Nikki, and I assured him that all the girl and I engaged in was intelligent conversations. I was sweating as I awaited my fate.

My crisis was averted when the man calmed down. He seemed to believe me, and had remarked that he thought that I might even be a decent young man. To my astonishment, Mr. Smith invited me to spend the night over at their home.

I packed a bag and went home with them. I slept in the guest room. Before going to sleep, Nikki came over to the room (the door was left ajar) and we spoke until her parents reminded her that it was bedtime. She obeyed and went to her room.

The following day, Saturday, Mr. Smith drove Nikki and me to the movies. He picked us up later, and I spent that night at the Smith's house in the guest room. Again Nikki slept in her room. Mr. Smith drove me home on Sunday evening.

Nikki and I developed a close friendship that her parents were fully aware of. I spent several weekends at their house in the guest room but we were never physically intimate. She telephoned me every day, and we had lengthy conversations. I enjoyed speaking with her, and looked forward to her phone calls.

One day Mrs. Smith phoned me and complained that her daughter's school grades were plummeting. Nikki's academic decline was attributed to our relationship. Her mother claimed that our daily phone calls were distracting her daughter from school work. Then Mrs. Smith asked me to end the relationship with Nikki. She knew that her daughter would not comply if she had asked her to end the relationship with me. I responded: "Yes ma'am."

That was the last conversation that I had with Nikki's mother. However from then on Nikki ignored her mother's command, and used the phone from one of her friends' house, to communicate with me. We continued to talk.

One day, Nikki asked if she could spend the weekend at my place. By then I had moved out from her friend, Cherry's house and had rented a room a few streets away. I had not anticipated that, and I wasn't ready for an intimate relationship with her.

I knew that Mr. and Mrs. Smith would not permit her to stay overnight at my place. Nikki told me that she had planned to tell them that she would be spending the weekend with relatives in New York, so there was no need for me to worry. Her parents would be none the wiser.

Although I liked her and felt flattered that she wanted to be intimate, I had no intention of risking my life - her father wouldn't hesitate to harm me - and I was not comfortable with the possibility of fatherhood. So, on the day that she planned to spend the weekend with me, I was nervous.

Before she arrived at my room, I left for my friend's house and never returned that day. When she came by and realized that I had left, she was very angry at me. I had stood her up! After that incident, Nikki stopped calling me and our friendship ended.

Four years went by as I continued to live and work in Poughkeepsie as a construction worker. My Boss was Ezekiel; he knew me as James Clark, and I called him Manager. The wages were reasonable. During that time, I had built friendships and developed a comfortable way of life. I worked hard, and played well. Weekends were reserved for bars and parties.

One day, John, my close friend, introduced me to the idea of selling marijuana as a way to supplement my income. I understood the risks of dealing with illegal drugs and the negative life-altering circumstances; moreover, if the authorities intercepted and I was caught, it would mean prison. However, the monetary promises were so lucrative that I found it very difficult to resist.

Eventually, I succumbed to the temptation and started to sell marijuana at my apartment. I bought it from the suppliers and resold it to users. When business started to flourish, I rented a three-bedroom house for the sole purpose of dealing drugs, ignoring the associated dangers. I continued living at my apartment, conscious that danger lurked.

A crude reminder of danger came one night while I was hanging out with my friends in the Bronx. My friend, John had invited me to hang out at his friend's apartment. We were in the midst of socializing, and smoking a few joints when the doorbell rang. One of the men in the room got up and went to the front door. As he looked through the peephole, shots rang out. The person outside the door shot him.

I realized that some of John's associates led more complicated lives. Some of them may have been associated with gangs. I, along with my visiting friends fled the building that night; I didn't know the guy who was shot. I was terrified, and didn't want to be part of that life on the edge. In the late nineteen sixties and early nineteen seventies, life in New York City was challenging, especially for young African-American men.

One rainy day, I stayed home from work on the advice of my boss. Due to the inclement weather we were unable to do construction work. It was a great break that afforded me a day of leisure. I joined my neighbour and a few friends in a game of dominoes – my favourite game. We played all day and ended at midnight. My landlord served kidney- bean soup.

The next day, on my way to collect wages from my boss, I was stopped by the police. They arrested me, and accused me of unlawful breaking, and entering a store the night before. Somehow, they reckoned that I had fit the profile of the wanted criminal. I was interrogated at the police division. I reiterated that I had nothing to do with the crime. They showed me a cash register, and asked if I recognized it.

Then I was asked to be part of a line-up, and two women from the store identified me as the person who broke the store. When given a phone call, I called my landlord. Thankfully, he was able to provide a credible alibi, because I was playing Dominoes on the same night that the crime had taken place. Eventually I was released. That was my first encounter with the police in the America.

Trouble seemed to follow me wherever I went. One night at a bar, I was in the process of ordering a beer when some random guy accused me of harassing the female bartender, whom he claimed was his girlfriend. His three friends surrounded me and started issuing threats. One of them knocked off my hat. Quietly, feeling humiliated, I picked up my hat, and left the bar.

When I got home, I felt angry, so I took a piece of pipe iron and returned to the bar. I approached the four men and challenged them to defend themselves as I launched an attack. I hit all four of them with the pipe iron, and quickly exited the bar. After the incident, I never returned to that bar.

Feeling beaten down and trapped, I started to reflect on my life and all of the fundamental values that my mother had instilled in me as a child while growing up in Jamaica. I cried, and prayed aloud.

As I pleaded to God for help, I made the promise to serve faithfully if I was spared imprisonment. I knew then that it was a great test of faith. I cried and prayed aloud to the annoyance of the others in the adjoining jail cells.

"Shut up!"

Ignoring their rebuke, I continued with my prayers and cries for help. A few days later, I was brought before the Judge.

The Judge asked how I pleaded. Realizing that it was my first, albeit serious offense, the Judge granted me bail for one hundred thousand U.S. dollars. I contacted a private company to get help with accessing bail. Eventually I was set free from jail until a new date was set for trial.

In preparation for my trial, I consulted a lawyer. He informed me that if convicted, my sentence could be between fifteen and twenty-five years in prison. He also told me that the cost to retain him for legal services would be approximately five thousand dollars.

Again, I reflected on my life and weighed the pros and cons. I didn't want to go to prison! I decided to seek help from relatives, when no solutions were forthcoming. In desperation, I decided to leave America.

Returning to Jamaica was not my preference so I decided that as a last resort, I would try to make my way up north to Canada. There I planned to turn a new page and make a fresh start. So, on that fateful day of spring, the season that represented renewal, I headed for Canada.

THERE, AT THE CANADIAN BORDER, I STOOD NERVOUS and uncertain as the Canadian immigration officer patiently awaited my signature sample. It was the final precondition to enter Canada, the country that represented hope.

As if by celestial obedience, I allowed my hand to scribble on the piece of paper that the immigration officer had handed me. With childlike faith, I gracefully surrendered to the outcome, whether my signature matched, or didn't match, the ID card.

Thankfully, miraculously, my nervous scribble was a perfect replica of the one on the ID card! The immigration officer then handed me my documents. With a warm smile that counteracted the freezing spring day, he greeted me: "Welcome to Canada!"

PART TWO

DEDICATED

TO

MY BROTHER

JOSHUA DOCKERY

CHAPTER NINE

"THANK YOU, SIR." I RESPONDED, AS I ACCEPTED THE document from the Canadian immigration officer. All was clear for me to cross the border into Canada. Words could not express how I felt.

My hands were still trembling. However, deep down inside, I felt a great sense of relief. I was overwhelmed with joy which was reminiscent of the day I learned that I was accepted to travel to work on the sugarcane plantation in Belle Glade, Florida. Then, I had no idea what awaited me in America, but I was certain that I wanted to leave Jamaica and the past behind. I had no plans then to travel to Canada, because I couldn't anticipate where my journey would lead to. So, there I was again, headed on another new journey that was filled with uncertainty; albeit joyful.

Suddenly, my joy changed to excitement, as I returned to the Greyhound bus. I was about to face passengers that were delayed because of me, but I was so preoccupied with my new reality that I shrugged off the concern. As we headed beyond the border I realized that this was not just another trip. Certainly, it was not an ordinary trip!

I thought that this was the opportunity of a lifetime. It was the trip that would take me away from the struggles in America. I reckoned that I was about to embark on *my journey to a better life*.

By the time I arrived at the bus terminal in downtown Toronto, I was exhausted and sleepy. The feeling of weariness was beyond tired joints from half day of sitting on the bus. My mind was restless from fear and over-thinking.

As I alighted from the Greyhound bus, there was so much to be thankful for, yet I was overwhelmed with trepidation. As I awaited the bus that would take me to the final leg of my journey, I succumbed to my weary eyes.

The next morning I boarded the bus to Sudbury, headed east. With renewed excitement and anticipation, I kept awake. My mind was formulating the correct words to inform my brother that I had arrived in Canada. Prior to leaving America, I had asked my brother to assist me. Although he was a permanent resident of Canada, he had made it clear that he was not in a position to help me. Furthermore, he was adamant that he was not going to collaborate with me to risk losing his Canadian status. He was opposed to using any fraudulent means to help me to cross the Canadian border.

As the bus approached my destination, I yawned in an effort to release the mixture of fear and excitement. In addition to my brother, I had other siblings and several relatives who by this time, resided in Canada. No one had any idea that I was about to join them. Briefly, I tried to anticipate how they would react to my presence. Surprise would be an understatement.

I pondered how I would explain my reason for fleeing America and, the process that I had chosen to cross the border into Canada. I wanted them to embrace me, and support my desperate efforts to settle into this new life. I wanted this chapter of my life to be better, and I was willing to do whatever it took to achieve the success that I had anticipated when I left Jamaica.

My stated reason for traveling to Canada was to attend my father's funeral, but my father was not dead. He lived in Jamaica. Choosing to start a new life in Canada was like burying the past, as I approached a future filled with hope.

CHAPTER TEN

Soon after I got off the bus at the Sudbury bus station, I headed for the nearest payphone booth. My fingers trembled with excitement as I dialed the number to my brother's house. Nervously, I listened to the ringing. My brother, Joshua answered the telephone.

I was happy to hear his voice, and I could hardly wait to break the news. Trying my best to sound calm, I asked him to pick me up at the bus terminal. Thinking that I was still in America, he reiterated that he couldn't help me to cross the border into Canada. Previously, when I had asked him to help me to cross the border, he had made it clear that he was not willing to participate in anything illegal.

Based on the way our mother had raised us, we were taught to always make the right choices, and to respect the family's name. I understood how making the choice to break the law or to take the risk of getting involved with any illegal activities would not be an option for my brother.

With confidence, I said: "I'm in Canada!"

There was a pause, and then with a voice of skepticism he replied: "What do you mean by you're in Canada?"

I repeated: "I'm in Canada!"

After another awkward pause he asked: "Where exactly are you?"

I responded: "I'm at the bus station in Sudbury."

With a sound of shock in his voice, my brother then exclaimed: "Are you kidding me?"

Once I convinced him that I was actually standing in a telephone booth in Sudbury, he assured me that he would come to meet me. Within twenty minutes Joshua met me at the bus station. I smiled at the look of utter shock on his face. On our way to his house, as he drove, he asked how I got to Canada.

I replied: "It's a long story."

He took me to his home, and immediately started calling my other siblings and relatives in Canada. As he broke the news of my sudden arrival, I could hear the surprise in his voice: "Guess who's here!"

By the end of that day, my siblings and several other relatives had gathered at my brother's house. They wasted no time in coming to Joshua's house. In hindsight I think that they had rushed to see me mostly out of inquisitiveness. They had to see for themselves, that truly I was on Canadian soil!

After they had established it was me, they seemed to be more curious to find out what method I had used to get through to arrive safely in Canada, because none of them had helped me. I divulged small excerpts of my journey from the time that I had left our family's home in the District of Haddo.

I filled them in on the choice I had made to run away to Montego Bay, and my journey to Florida to work on the sugarcane plantations. They were also curious to know about my experiences living in America.

Notwithstanding their curiosity, I gave them only a few snippets of my life in America. I withheld details about how I got over the border to arrive in Canada. For the most part, evidenced by their hugs, laughter and smiles, they all seemed happy to see me, alive and well. After the spontaneous meeting with my siblings and relatives, I left my brother's house and went to live with my sister.

Realizing that I was in a new country, my priority was to gather as much pertinent information as possible in order to familiarize myself with a new way of life. My biggest dilemma was how to start without legal documents to work in Canada, I was afraid to reveal my true identity. I decided to take on a new name and persona. I chose the name Dave Carrington. Masking the old Handel, in order to face my new life, I introduced myself to everyone as: Dave.

Under the pseudonym Dave Carrington, I then applied for a Social Insurance Number, which was a legal identification card that was needed for employment and taxes. In the application, Dave stated that his place of birth was Nova Scotia, Canada, and also came up with names for his parents who resided in Nova Scotia. I had no knowledge of where in Canada the province of Nova Scotia was located then. Shortly after I filed the application, a Social Insurance Number, was mailed to me.

Everyone outside my family, and even some family members called me Dave. With a Social Insurance Number, I was able to work 'legally.'

CHAPTER ELEVEN

I LIVED AT MY SISTER'S HOUSE FOR ABOUT A YEAR, while I tried desperately to find employment. My first job in Canada was working in construction, finishing cement, and laying tiles. I worked long hours finishing concrete floors. My first boss was a fast-talking Italian man; he took advantage of me by paying me less than the minimum wage.

Although the basic wage for a non-unionized finisher then was $15.00 an hour, my boss paid me only $5.00 an hour. However, I was thankful to have a job. I worked with him while I searched for a job that would pay me more money.

Then, I heard that one of the hospitals was hiring in the housekeeping department. I applied and was very optimistic that I would be offered a position because I was confident that I could do that job. Moreover, I had a good contact who worked at that hospital.

I was happy when I got a phone call to attend a job interview. However, after the job interview, a staff in the Human Resources Department of the hospital requested a copy of my birth certificate as identification; it was a prerequisite for employment. I had no birth certificate for Dave Carrington! Disappointed with not being hired by the hospital, I continued to work for my exploitive Italian boss.

Growing up in Jamaica, my family never owned a car; not even a bicycle. I desperately wanted to own a car. One day, I saw a used car for sale; I purchased it for $100. Never mind it was a used car; Dave was the proud owner of a Chrysler!

By Jamaican standards, being a car owner was a great accomplishment. After I bought the car, I had it towed to the apartment where I lived with my girlfriend.

Judy was my first girlfriend in Canada. She was a beautiful, blonde, blue-eyed Canadian young woman whose parents had emigrated from Finland. She was the mother of a three-month-old baby when we met. At that time, she lived in Hamilton.

I met Judy at a Disco party. At that time, she was visiting her mother, who resided in Sudbury. While at the party, she was seated at a table with her four girlfriends. I observed that her friends were dancing but she stayed seated at the table. I mustered up the courage, and asked her to dance. She agreed, and we danced to a slow song.

I whispered to her as we danced. I told her that I thought she was beautiful. We danced for the rest of the night, and when the party was over, she accepted my offer to walk her home. That night, before we parted ways, she gave me her telephone number.

After that night, Judy and I saw each other often. She lived in Hamilton, and I lived in Sudbury. As we dated, I grew madly in love with her. Soon afterward she left Hamilton; I helped her with the move. We got a new apartment in Sudbury, and moved in together. After two years we were officially engaged with plans to get married. My brother Joshua hosted our engagement party at his house.

I continued to seek employment with a better salary. One day, I found out that my Italian boss was charging his clients $25.00 an hour for the jobs while he paid me $5.00 an hour for doing the work. I became upset! I decided that I could no longer allow him to take advantage of me. I'd had enough, so I walked off the job.

Just the thought of being unemployed was overbearing, and helped to fuel my frustration. That morning after I walked off the job, I went home to my fiancée. We argued about something silly. As the argument escalated I become more upset, but I did not want to be involved with a physical fight with her. I stormed out of the apartment.

In a fit of rage I decided to take a ride in my car. I felt the need to get away for a while to cool down. It was a hot summer day, and that didn't help. Although I had no drivers' license, and the car was not insured, I decided to take the risk anyway.

I started to drive and shortly afterward, I realized that the brakes of the car were faulty. After I used the accelerator, it became very difficult to control the wheel. That was scary!

As I drove around the corner, two streets away from my apartment, my car spun out of control. Within seconds, I hit the back of a parked car! The impact of the accident made a loud noise which drew the attention of the neighbours on the street. As a crowd started to gather to investigate the accident, I became scared. Confused, I abandoned my car and took off running.

CHAPTER TWELVE

I HAD HIT THE BACK OF A BRAND NEW CAR; IT WAS A Lincoln Continental. Then, I had fled the scene of the accident. Several witnesses and persons who came out to investigate the noise were able to identify me. The police was notified. That incident was my first interaction with the police in Canada.

I sweated buckets as I headed to the nearest telephone booth. The police had put out an All Points Bulletin with my description. They were on the hunt to catch me because I was responsible for the accident.

I called my brother Joshua, and informed him of the accident. Joshua instructed me to stay put. Shortly afterward, he came to the phone booth to pick me up. Joshua told me that he was making a 'citizen's arrest.' He asked me to get into his car, and drove me to the police station. I was fearful, to say the least; my brother seemed very serious, and I was unsure about what the consequences of my action would be. My own brother had placed me under arrest. I was shocked!

Joshua explained that he was driving me to the police station to take responsibility for the hit and run, the result of my poor choices. I knew that it was wrong to drive a vehicle without a valid driver's license. To make matters worse, the car was not insured.

Fortunately, my brother understood the legal system. Also, Joshua was a well known ally to the Sudbury police due to his work in a senior security capacity.

At the police station, Joshua requested to speak with the Chief. He then brought me into the Chief's office and told him that he made a citizen's arrest for the man who was wanted for the hit and run accident. He introduced me, the culprit, as his brother.

I was issued two tickets for traffic violation: one ticket was for driving without a license, and the other was for driving a vehicle that was not insured. I was also charged with failing to remain at the scene of the accident. However, with Joshua's intervention, and support, I was able to leave the police station that day.

The All Points Bulletin was called off. That was a close call! I felt indebted to Joshua. Not all the members of my family were supportive.

Later, I was told that the news of my accident had stirred strong discussion, gossip, and opinions among some of my relatives. One of my relatives had expressed disappointment in my behaviour and had disagreed with Joshua for supporting me.

Apparently a member of family deemed my behaviour as a major source of disgrace. That relative wanted the police to apprehend me, and put me through the legal system, and even deport me to Jamaica.

One of my relatives had viewed my behaviour as an embarrassment to the Dockery family, and a disrespect of my mother, who had recently immigrated to Canada. It was seen as spoiling the family's name. As children, my mother had taught us to "always respect the family's name."

In 1976, my mother had obtained landed status, and immigrated to Canada. That was a memorable year - the year when the CN Tower opened. Then, it was the tallest freestanding structure in the world. It was also the year that Canada abolished the death penalty.

My mother had lived a quiet life in Canada, and spent time assisting with raising her grandchildren. She lived with my brother Joshua, and my other siblings. She lived with me for about a year, and during that time, we established a very strong bond. I was her pastor, and confidant. Later, she resided in her own apartment in a seniors' building.

CHAPTER THIRTEEN

THAT BRUSH WITH THE AUTHORITIES HAD SERVED AS a serious life lesson. The "reckless" driving incident spurred my determination to refocus, and find employment.

After I had walked off the job where I worked with my Italian boss, I had decided to start my own business. I went to a printing shop and bought business cards. The name of my new business was 'Dave's Cement & Tile.'

Being a person of African ancestry, it was difficult to get into the construction management business. At that time, the construction industry was dominated by Italians and Portuguese.

Nonetheless, I distributed my business cards. At first, I got no positive responses, and no jobs, but I was adamant that I would keep trying, even without support from others.

It was challenging to deal with a lot of rejection, but I was determined not to succumb to failure. Intuitively, I knew that it was possible to overcome the challenges.

Some of my relatives and friends discouraged me. Despite this, my goal was to become a successful entrepreneur. I knew that I had to think creatively, and remain strong-willed if I had to overcome ongoing rejections.

One day I decided to approach a builder with an unusual proposal. In my research, I found out that this man was planning to build houses. So, with all the confidence I could muster, I negotiated to do work on the first house for free.

As part of our mutual agreement, if the quality of my work met his satisfaction, the builder would give me the contract for the remainder of the houses. I had to work on the first house, and create my best impression.

That impression would be the first for Dave's Cement and Tiles! I set my goal to do an excellent job, by any means necessary in order to please the builder. Dave's Cement and Tile had no assets or inventory. Without a vehicle or any equipment it seemed almost impossible to start working on the first house.

However, I focused on solutions instead of obstacles. I went to a lumber yard, and bought lumber and plywood to construct tools to pour the concrete. I was able to carry the concrete mix to the basement through a window. I then rented a power trowel and a small car. With tenacity, I had set out to make my proposal a success.

CHAPTER FOURTEEN

LANDING THAT CONTRACT WOULD GIVE ME A GREAT break, although I would have no monetary gain. It was very hard work! That relatively small car, a Hornet, had limited capacity but I tied the equipment on the roof and secured the trowel in the truck of the car with a rope.

Fortunately, I was not stopped by police, as I drove around in a car with what could be considered hazardous obstructing lumber. I had to do all the work alone because I could not afford to employ someone to help me.

It was extremely difficult to lift the power trowel by myself. At the end of some days I had to crawl around on the floor because of pains in my legs, back, and all over my body. It felt torturous, but I refused to quit.

As I laboured all alone I reflected on the old belief back on the island of Jamaica, that the streets in foreign lands were paved with gold. It was a myth! I also knew that opportunities existed for those who were willing to work hard. Sometimes a job required more than just physical efforts.

I struggled to complete the job, but I knew that it would pay off if I didn't give up. Eventually I completed the first house successfully. The contractor was very pleased with my work. He honoured my proposal and gave me the contract to complete the other houses.

That contract propelled the new business of Dave's Cement and Tile. I was able to use that job as reference to my work when I sought other concrete and tile jobs. Soon, I became known as the 'black Italian.'

I continued to work and was able to hire one employee. We progressed until I hired five employees. Then I bought a truck. I got my driver's license in my birth name – Handel Dockery. That was the first time in years since I had used my birth name. Business was flourishing with Dave's Concrete and Tile Company.

My business was established, and I was contented. Again, I was offered an opportunity to deal in illegal drugs. This time I refused! Instead, I thought about my promise to God, and decided to attend church. I attended The First Baptist church.

Judy accepted the invitation to attend church with me. Although this was her first time at church, my fiancée decided to take communion. I discouraged her from doing so, but she dismissed it as 'just a piece of bread and wine.'

It upset me that she disregarded the symbol of bread and wine at church. I tried to explain the significance of communion. I told Judy that I had planned to continue going to church to 'put my life in order.'

Judy and I argued about religion, and she told me that she didn't want to be involved in church. Later, I found out that she was having a relationship with another man. I broke off the engagement; she kept the diamond ring.

Single again, I rented a room; it was in a private house – the landlady was a Jehovah Witness. No sooner than I became her tenant, she began preaching to me. She invited me to service at her church the Kingdom Hall of Jehovah Witness.

Every Saturday she conducted a Bible study group and I joined her. Then I began attending church with her every Sunday. I got deeply involved in the church – I began to give talks.

During Bible study we disagreed on some topics. I realized that we had differing explanations regarding concepts of heaven and hell. To become a Witness I had to be baptized. I refused to be baptized.

Meanwhile, I had fallen in love with a young woman from the church; she was a Witness and we wanted to get married. In order to get married I had to get baptized. Our religious differences made it difficult to continue the relationship. One morning, I visited her at her job to inform her that I could no longer continue the relationship with her.

Although I was making the decision based on my belief, it was heartbreaking because I had really loved her. Shortly after I stopped attending the Jehovah Witness church, I joined a Pentecostal church.

CHAPTER FIFTEEN

WHILE ATTENDING THE PENTECOSTAL CHURCH I MET Nancy. She was part of our youth social circle that met for discussion and board games on weekends. At that time I was in a relationship with another young woman. Initially Nancy ignored me, but later she became my friend and confidant.

My personal life was complicated, to say the least. In fact that aspect of my journey is part of another story for another book. Nancy and I got married. After we got married I decided that it was time to take charge of my life, and to pursue legal immigration status in Canada.

One morning, I went to an immigration office. I told one of the officers that my birth name was Handel Dockery, and that I wished to apply for landed immigrant status in Canada.

The immigration officer searched for my name in the computer; there were no records. When he asked what my country of origin was; I told him Jamaica. He accused me of lying.

He said that there was no record of my point of entry into Canada. He enquired what my point of entry was. I refused to divulge that information because it was his job to find out. I thought if I had told him, he would become wise to that loophole. In the event that someone else tried to use that loophole as I did, their chances would be jeopardized.

I did not provide the information. Knowing that as a young man back in Jamaica how much I was desperate to leave, I didn't want to hamper the opportunity of someone else who would probably seek to travel like I did.

The immigration officer realized that I was an alien but he could not identify me for deportation purposes. He put me in a holding room and started to interrogate me. I felt secured at the time having lived in Canada for five years, with an established business, five employees and legally married.

The immigration officer asked if I was married. I replied 'yes.' I then asked for a phone call and called my wife. Nancy came to the Immigration centre, and after she verified that we were married, the officer released me.

I disclosed my phone number and address to the officer. He also asked my country of birth. Later, he contacted the Jamaican High Commissioner. In their research, they were able to verify that I was born in Jamaica.

A few weeks after, the immigration gave me an appointment. I returned and filled out an application for a Jamaican passport. I received the passport and then applied for landed status in Canada. I then surrendered the fake Social Insurance Card that was in the name of Dave Carrington, and I was issued a new Social Insurance Number.

From then I was able to live, and work freely using an authentic Social Insurance Number. It felt as though a burden had been lifted off my shoulders, like a newly found freedom.

Anxious to share the great news, I called my old boss Ezekiel, in Poughkeepsie, New York. He was my last employer when I worked in construction years ago. As his apprentice, he not only taught me the technicalities of the concrete trade, he was like a big brother. I wanted to keep in touch and let him know how life was for me since I left New York. Back then, I was known by the alias James Clarke.

Ezekiel's wife, Vivian answered the phone: "Hello?"

"Hi Vivian, this is James."

"James who?"

I answered, "James Clarke."

With a surprised and animated voice she said: "Stop! Don't do that; you know James is dead, why are you doing that?"

She kept repeating, as if in shock: "Who is it? Who is it?"

I replied: "It's me, James."

Then she called her husband: "Ezekiel! Ezekiel! Come here! There is some idiot on the phone saying that he is James."

Ezekiel took the phone: "Hello?"

I replied: "Hello Ezekiel."

In a stern voice, he asked: "Who is it?"

"This is James, James Clark."

"James who?" he asked, sounding agitated.

Calmly, I repeated: "James Clark."

"Stop that! Who is it?"

"James Clarke."

I had known Ezekiel as a calm person who never yelled or cursed, but when he got upset at his employees he would always use a phrase in Jamaican patois to express anger: "Wish-a-part!"

On the job I had always referred to Ezekiel as 'Manager.'

When I realized that he was upset, I said: "Manager."

Then he paused and asked again in a calm manner, "Who is this?"

I replied, "James, James Clark."

"You can't be James; James is dead."

"I'm not dead; I'm James, and I'm living in Canada"

Ezekiel had a reaction of upset and shock to my phone call because he thought that I had died, and someone was being an impersonator - disrespectful to "James Clark."

He asked: "Do you know what happened to John?"

John was my friend who had introduced me to marijuana in New York. He had invited me to that party in the Bronx, where his friend was shot through the keyhole. I replied: "No."

He told me that John had died. I was shocked as I paused to absorb the news.

I asked: "What do you mean?"

Now, realizing that I was alive, he proceeded to tell me that John went to the Bronx and found another friend to help with the business of selling marijuana. As the business grew they had dissentions with other drug dealers. One Saturday night, they got into a gun fight, and John was killed.

The killer had pulled the trigger in the mouth of John's partner, shattering his brain. That made it impossible to identify him. John and I were friends, and I had no identification when I was in New York. The assumption was made that I was killed.

A funeral was held with the understanding that I had passed, evidenced by a grave in Poughkeepsie. I felt very sorrowful for my friend John and I was thankful that I was not his friend who was killed.

Nancy and I remained married for sixteen years. We had two sons and two daughters. I am alive today by God's grace.

CHAPTER SIXTEEN

DURING THE RECESSION OF 1981, CONTRACTS IN THE construction industry were few, and the number of jobs declined. With fewer contracts, I was forced to downsize business and eventually, I had to lay off my employees.

I then sought other employment and found job as a lumberjack in Northern Ontario. The cabin that we lived in was so small that it could not even accommodate a refrigerator; we stored perishable food in a container inside the window.

The weather was extremely cold, so I decided to seek employment in another field! When I returned to Sudbury, I saw a newspaper clipping advertising vacancies with a company in London, in southern Ontario. The company COFO was looking for cement finishers. Together with a friend, I traveled to London. It was my first visit to London, Ontario, and I had no place to live.

Shortly after we got off the Greyhound bus I met Mary, a Jamaican lady who lived in London, Ontario. I greeted her and we got into a casual conversation. Somehow she recognized me as a stranger to the area. In a friendly manner, she asked what I was doing in London. I told her that I was there to seek employment, but I had no place to stay.

Mary invited me to stay at her house. She introduced me to her husband and children. She treated me as family. The next day I found the company COFO, and I was hired as a cement finisher.

I felt very lucky to be employed and to have a comfortable place to stay. Mary and her European husband invited me to stay at their home. She prepared breakfast every morning, and packed lunch for me. Dinner was served every evening. To my astonishment, Mary refused to accept payment from me for boarding and meals.

Everyday at the table we said Grace before meals. One day Mary asked if I was a Christian, and I replied 'yes.' She asked how I was baptized. Although we had a dissention about baptism, she always invited me to attend her church. Consistently, I declined her invitation.

Sometimes my wife, Nancy, visited on the weekend, and we would rent a motel room. Later I rented an apartment. I was very grateful for the hospitality of Mary and her family. Upon leaving, I thanked Mary, and I told her I'd do anything for her. Mary told that me that she would be pleased if I attended her church.

To fulfill my promise, one Sunday I accepted Mary's invitation, and attended her church. My intention was to satisfy that one desire which she had expressed repeatedly, while I stayed at her home. I had no expectations other than to please Mary by sitting in at the service.

On that Sunday, to my surprise, the church service marked a major turning point in my life. After water baptism I had a vision through a dream. That vision changed my life! It was a recurring dream: visions, and prayers that were precursors to my life. However, that is another story to tell when I write about the spiritual leg of my life's journey.

I attributed that visit to Mary's church to later being motivated to pursue studies at Bible College. I then studied theology full time, for two years at the Apostolic Missionary Institute (AMI) in London Ontario. When I completed studies, I returned to Sudbury.

Then I went to work in the uranium mine in Elliot Lake for a year. After working in the mine, I applied to the government for a student loan to attend university. I was also awarded a forgivable loan. Meanwhile, I opened a Coffee shop in Sudbury. My specialties were coffee, tea, sandwiches, burgers, and fries. I hired two employees. Later, I sold the coffee shop.

I attended Laurentian University in greater Sudbury, with the intention of becoming a lawyer. Without adequate support, and being the only student of colour in my class, studying was a huge challenge. When I started school, I was assessed to be with second year students, so I was off to a slow start because I did not have the foundation of the first year. Sadly I didn't complete university and didn't graduate therefore I didn't attend law school.

Then, I moved to Kingston, Ontario, east of Toronto (capital of Ontario) and opened up a business selling Rainbow vacuum cleaners. I hired twenty employees as telemarketers to make phone calls, and set up appointments for the Sales Representatives.

The Sales Representatives, whom I hired on commission, would visit potential customers that were contacted by the telemarketers. I owned and managed that business for five years.

When the market waned in the sales of vacuum cleaners, I closed the shop and returned to work in the construction field. I then opened an office in Hamilton. The construction contracts were mainly house repairs. Later I closed that business, and went to work with TRIDEL as a concrete finisher.

There was another drastic decline in construction jobs. Workers in the union could not work for private companies. Again, I had to find a way to earn enough income to support my wife and children. Nancy and I had four children.

One day, I went to the north of Toronto, in the town of Richmond Hill. I found a wholesale business that sold roses; the prices were reasonable and I thought of testing the retail market for roses. I bought twelve dozens roses at whole sale price.

I went from door to door and sold all the roses. My profit margin was great, so I opened up a company called Roses & More. With my vehicle, I drove to various businesses and sold roses to many individuals. That's how I was able to have an income to take care of my family.

Later I worked for a company selling a cleaning product (Urad); it was a type of creamy material used for cleaning leather. Special kiosks were set up in Malls and major department stores (Sears, The Bay, and Eaton's) to sell the products. When customers were shopping, my job was to approach them and demonstrate how the product was used to clean, and protect leather items. I was paid by commission; I earned an average of $5 per sale.

After a few months, my sales increased, and I was promoted to the position of manager. I supervised staff in various kiosks and trained new staff. My job was to impart knowledge about the product, and to motivate staff. I was also appointed as the liaison between the company's head office and the kiosks.

Once I understood how the business model worked, I resigned from being a manager and became a distributor. I owned kiosks, and participated in tradeshows all across Canada and the United States. Tradeshows, especially in the USA were challenging. I hired salespeople in the USA and Canada. I traveled extensively throughout the USA.

Due to racial discrimination, sometimes I dreaded traveling in some parts of the USA. Traveling was high risk, especially when I chose to sleep in my car. During those times, I would cover up with a blanket to hide myself. My wife was very scared for my safety when I traveled alone.

CHAPTER SEVENTEEN

IN THE SPRING OF APRIL 1 1973, I HAD ARRIVED IN Canada with two suits of clothing, and a dream. It was my desire to improve my life so that my journey would be fulfilling. Canada provided me with valuable opportunities, and a place to proudly call home. I was able to leave my old life behind and embark on an amazing journey.

Then, on Saturday, September 7th, 1985 at about 3 a.m., I was awakened by a phone call; it was my mother. When I answered the phone that sweet, tender voice said: "Son, please come; I'm dying."

Scared and shocked I nervously jumped into my truck and drove to her apartment. When I opened the door my mother was standing in front of the mirror combing her hair. She had taken a shower, and was dressed nicely.

I said, "Hi mom." She turned her head, looked at me with a smile, and immediately fell backwards. Quickly, I stretched out my arms in the nick of time to catch her.

Slowly, I lowered her to the floor, and dialed 911. Kneeling beside to her, I prayed. The ambulance arrived shortly after, and transported her to the hospital. I drove behind the ambulance to the hospital.

When we arrived there I began making phone calls to my siblings. I waited patiently and watched as the doctors attended to my mother. She laid there and watched as her children appeared one by one. As each one came into the room she held up one finger until the last came.

Then she breathed her last breath, and bid the world goodbye. I was in shock and awe; we all were. We had lost our beloved mom. She was only 68 years of age.

Often, I have reflected on my mother's life - her strength, and courage, have been exemplary. Despite the hardships which she endured, my mother had continued to help others with her head kept high.

Currently, in my career as a Personal Support Worker (PSW), I am pleased to provide a high standard of care to persons who have served this country, and through their contributions, helped so that I was able to get a chance of a new life. I think that it is my duty to serve the sick, weak, and vulnerable as a way of giving back to the society that has given a great deal to me.

Before I became a Personal Support Worker, I had a deep desire to positively impact the lives of others. Participating actively in church was great; I also chose to minister from door to door, and invited people to church. That was fulfilling, but the outcome was not always good.

Many doors were slammed in my face. I endured insults, but one of the most frightening challenges I faced happened one Saturday morning. That day, I got up, as usual, had my breakfast, prayed and left my house to invite people to church. As I knocked on this particular door, a lady came to the door.

She was very slim, about fifty-five years of age, with long, untidy-looking hair. I greeted her and introduced myself. Then I asked her:

"Do you know the Lord Jesus Christ as your personal Saviour?"

She gave me a daring stare, then pulled a long shotgun and pointed it in my face. She yelled, "I'm going to blow your head off!"

I was frozen for a moment or so. Then I raised my right hand and responded:

"In the name of Jesus Christ, put down that gun!"

She held the gun for a short while before putting it away. I felt relieved. I left her a brochure to read, and continued with my evangelism.

I attended training in Texas. Later, I opened a Christian school in Hamilton - the Mount Olive Christian Academy - for grades 1 to 12.

The alternate curriculum, approved by the Ministry of Education, catered for the academic level of each individual child with assistance from trained educators. There, I felt like I impacted the lives of many children. I had made a promise to God and I deeply wanted to realize that promise.

I attended a theological college and devoted myself to studying the word of God. God changed me from a sinner, a lawbreaker, a bitter person - one would even say a criminal - to a God-fearing law-abiding citizen, who contributed and continues to contribute to society by helping those who are vulnerable.

Currently, I am also a minister of the Gospel, preaching the Gospel of Jesus Christ, telling the world and everyone reading this book that God is real. God changes lives. I know this to be true because I was a sinner, vile as vile could be, but when I accepted Jesus Christ as my personal Saviour and repented of my sins, He cleansed me.

Today I am not who I used to be, as the things I used to do, I no longer do. My testimony to everyone is that God changed me, and He can change you too; He will save you, if you allow Him to.

As you have taken this time to read my story, I hope and pray that your life may be touched and that you, too, will seek the Lord before it's too late. God bless you, and thank you for reading my book.

Getting back into church was an excellent choice. In hindsight, my journey thus far, and the manner in which my story unfolded, can be attributed to divine intervention. I truly believe that God had a hand in the events of my life.

For the most part, I almost always have a cheerful, optimistic disposition. I don't let things get to me, so I rarely frown. My only regret is the poor choice that I made in my youth, to get involved in the sale of illegal drugs. I don't drink alcohol, save for an occasional glass of wine.

When I was about sixteen years old I used to hang out with older men who drank alcohol while we played dominoes. I always drank soda. The men teased me, and told me that I was a 'baby'- not a man. They persistently dared me to 'be a man' by drinking alcohol.

Finally, I decided to prove to them that I was a man, not a 'baby.' One night I accepted the dare, and I drank rum and beer. I got drunk! I couldn't walk home, so I slept in an abandoned container.

Needless to say, I was very sick the next day. I regretted the choice to consume alcohol. Since then, that experience served as a life lesson. As I matured, I learned to sip a glass of wine. However, I don't drink any hard liquor or beer.

I know, without a doubt, that persistency, honesty and integrity build character. As a child, my mother often remarked that it was difficult to tell if I was upset or happy. I gained the nickname: 'laughy'.

Throughout my life, despite my trials, I have never given up. I have looked at obstacles as stepping stones. I realized that strong determination was needed to succeed.

I made strong efforts to learn lessons from my mistakes. That tenacity was instilled by my mother, since I was a child. I was determined to improve my life from the time I left Jamaica.

Whenever I became fearful or frustrated, I used faith, and willpower to keep going. I believed that the only time I could experience failure was when I stopped trying.

My aspiration to succeed was always strong. My strongest desire was to take care of myself and my family, and to be a positive role model. I wanted my children to become productive, independent citizens.

As long as I have good health I will keep active and take the opportunity to be part of any project that grabs my interest. I will be available for speaking engagements. God bless you, and thank you for reading the story of my journey thus far.

EPILOGUE

IT WAS A LONELY FEELING GROWING UP WITHOUT A father, even though my mother was very stern, and did an excellent job in parenting us. I always had that feeling of inferiority when I was among my playmates.

In my neighbourhood, it seemed that every child, except me, had a mom and dad; that seemed unfair. As a child, I was unable to express how growing up without my father impacted my life. I always harboured resentment which lingered into adulthood.

I reminisce about my very first girlfriend; her dad forbade her from talking to me. He had told her to stay away from me, because he had the belief that I would treat his daughter in the same manner that my dad treated my mother. So, there was that stigma which seemed to hang over me.

As an adult, after I got married and had children, I encountered challenging situations that could have been justification to dissolve my marriage. However, I always felt that I did not want to repeat my father's pattern, and leave my children without a father.

Today, I observe the same poor behaviour from other men who father children, especially among men of African Ancestry. Those men should realize that it takes more than dispersing a seed to be a father. It is our responsibility to take care of our children by nurturing them, and modeling how to be a man. I never had a desire to be like my father, but rather to be like my mother.

My second marriage was to a lady who had two sons. Her ex-husband, a Caucasian male, had abandoned her and their children; the boys had no relationship with their dad. I helped to raise them. My goal was to help break the cycle of absenteeism.

My father had abandoned his family, and had been living with his new wife, but he was still legally married to my mother. With no support from him, she had raised her children as a single parent.

A few weeks before her death in 1985, my mother had returned to Jamaica; she had expressed an eagerness to visit her home country again. During that visit she searched for my father.

On her return to Canada, she had told me and my siblings that she had found our dad. She talked about the deplorable conditions that my father lived in. During her visit to Jamaica, she had rented a place for him to live, and had opened a bank account in his name. Later, she had expressed that despite the way he had treated her, she wanted her children to support him. She had advocated that after all, he was still our father.

The passing away of my mother hit me very hard. She had complained previously of chest pains, and after taking her to the emergency, she was diagnosed as having a mild heart attack. However, as far as I knew, she was fine. Her passing had been sudden because I was unprepared.

After her death, we had followed mom's wishes to provide financial support to our father. My siblings and I assisted him until his passing in 2004, at the age of ninety-eight years. I was privileged to be the official preacher at his funeral.

To my fellowmen across Jamaica, Canada, the United States, and the globe (whether or not you are of African Descent), I encourage you to take care of your children. It is time for men to take the responsibility of parenting because their role of parenting is crucial to the future of humanity.

ACKNOWLEDGMENTS

I EXTEND SINCEREST THANKS TO MY BROTHERS Joshua, Felix, James, and Phillip who encouraged me to write this book. They were there for me when times were tough.

Wholeheartedly, I thank my sister, Annet who took me in when I came to Canada. She helped me a great deal on this journey.

Thanks to my wife of over twenty years. To my mother-in-law Carol, I thank you for your inspiration.

Special thanks to all my children: Natasha, Marc, Andre, Desiree, Jacinthe, Christopher, and Shamonique. I am proud of you, and I love you all unconditionally.